OBJECT PERMANENCE

OBJECT PERMANENCE

Poems

NICA BENGZON

Copyright © 2021 Nica Bengzon

Published by Gaudy Boy LLC,
an imprint of Singapore Unbound
www.singaporeunbound.org/gaudyboy
New York

For more information on ordering books, contact jkoh@singaporeunbound.org.

All rights reserved. No part of this publication may be reproduced or transmitted in any form or by any means without the prior written permission of the publisher, except for brief excerpts for the purpose of criticism and review.

ISBN: 978-0-9994514-3-4

Cover design by Flora Chan
Interior design by Jennifer Houle
Proofread by Cindy Hochman of "100 Proof" Copyediting Services

For my family.

And for Justine, to whom all my words go home.

CONTENTS

I

In the Event of a Catastrophe / 1

Active Listening / 15

The Law of Impenetrability / 17

An Inventory / 19

Object Permanence / 21

The Law of Gravity / 23

La Niña / 25

Lazarus Jewel Box / 27

The Law of Conservation / 29

God Never Blinks / 31

In Statu Viatoris / 33

II

Eating Disorder Not Otherwise Specified / 37

Anaphylaxis / 43

Metastasis / 45

Parasomnia / 47

Hypervigilance / 49

In Statu Viatoris / 51

A Miracle Story / 53

Shoot the Messenger / 57

Active Listening / 59

All Things Bright and Beautiful / 61

III

In Statu Viatoris / 67

Today We Are Canceling the Apocalypse / 69

Active Listening / 77

Breaking News / 81

As the Storyteller / 83

Scattering / 85

Surgery / 89

Pagpag / 91

True Facts About the Sea Turtle / 93

The Heart of the Blue Whale / 95

Origin Stories / 97

IV

Concerning *Object Permanence* as a
Poetry of Investigation: Marginalia / 105

Acknowledgments / 117

About the Author / 119

About Gaudy Boy / 121

OBJECT PERMANENCE

I

IN THE EVENT OF A CATASTROPHE

Victims of an event producing multiple human casualties must be sorted based on objective criteria, such as the severity of their injuries and their priority level for treatment and/or transport. Triage tags do this sorting by color code, so treatment and transport crews can see at a glance which patients have been triaged to which level. Learn to triage patients in a rapid but effective way, and you will do the greatest good for the greatest number of injured.

1. Conduct a scene size-up.
    a. Assure the well-being of responding medical personnel. Is the scene safe? If not, is it possible for you to render the scene safe before entering?
    b. Your personal safety is paramount in this operation. You can do nothing about the already-existent victims. You must not create more victims.

2. Take body substance isolation (BSI) precautions.
    a. Protect yourself from all body substances (blood, urine, feces, tears, etc.) of individuals undergoing medical treatment.
    b. Types of BSI include hospital gowns, medical gloves, shoe covers, surgical masks, and safety glasses.
    c. The aim is to reduce, as much as possible, the chance of transmitting any possible illnesses. Likewise, workers must be isolated from pathogens.

3. Determine the number of patients. If there are multiple (that is, there is more than one patient) or mass (that is, the number of patients exceeds the number of immediate care providers) casualties, communicate this through the appropriate channels, establish command, identify a medical officer and triage officer. Know all you encounter by name.
    a. Be as precise as possible in the communications. Provide a number, even an estimate. The actual number can be updated as more detailed information becomes available, or as more victims are found.
    b. In these instances, everyone must be accountable to someone else for the people they are holding. These people must be distributed according to their roles. It is clarity that keeps us alive in the event of disaster—who is victim, who is patient, who is casualty, who are medic and paramedic, to whom are all these people meant to answer? Who asks all the questions?

4. Clear out the "walking wounded."
    a. Simply announce *if any of you are well enough to stand and walk out of here, do so now.* Do not let these people wander aimlessly; direct them to an area of refuge. These victims are to be categorized GREEN: not requiring immediate attention.
    b. If you believe some of the uninjured victims are capable of assisting you, keep them near you to help if needed.

Now all you should be left with are those who cannot stand and
    walk on their own.
Who do you go to first?
The loudest?
The bloodiest?
The youngest?

5. Start where you stand. Regardless of what is going on around you, assess the first patient you encounter first. Triage with the head, not the heart—emotion can encumber analysis and hinder swift action.

a. Check for the presence of respiration.
    i. No respirations. Still none after you open their airway. Tag BLACK, for deceased.
    ii. No respirations. Respirations restored after correcting airway problems. Tag RED, for requiring immediate attention.
    iii. Respirations present. Respiratory rate above thirty breaths per minute. Tag RED, for requiring immediate attention.
    iv. Respirations present. Respiratory rate below thirty breaths per minute. Move on to assess perfusion criteria.

b. Evaluate the patient's pulse and capillary refill by applying pressure to the nail beds while the hand is held above the heart. Monitor how long it takes for blood to return to the tissue once the pressure has been released.
    i. Radial pulse is absent and capillary refill takes over two seconds. Tag RED, for requiring immediate attention.
    ii. Radial pulse is present and capillary refill takes under two seconds. Move on to assess mental status.

c. Assess the patient's mental status.
	i. The patient cannot follow simple commands (*Look at me. Say your name. Squeeze my hand if you can hear this.*) due to unconsciousness or an altered mental state. Tag RED, for requiring immediate attention.
	ii. The patient can follow simple commands. Tag YELLOW—their medical treatment may be delayed.

Remember that if your patient falls into the RED tag category on your first assessment, stop and tag them before moving on to another patient.

Do not attempt to correct any problems besides an obstructed airway or uncontrolled bleeding.

For this you may be able to use the capable "walking wounded"—have them maintain head position to keep an open airway, or apply consistent direct pressure to a large wound.

These people should be protected from exposure to blood and other bodily fluids.

6. Now that the patients have been triaged, more focused treatment can begin.
    a. Those tagged RED are treated, or moved to treatment areas first, followed by those tagged YELLOW.
    b. Patients tagged BLACK can be covered, if necessary, and left in place.

Further assessment of your patients will be done at various treatment areas as they are deployed on-scene. Patients need to be monitored in their treatment area(s) for changes in their conditions. Patients can be up-triaged or down-triaged as their conditions dictate.

> There are those who are likely to live,
> regardless of what care they receive.
> There are those who are likely to die,
> regardless of what care they receive.

> There are those for whom immediate
> care might make a positive difference.

Ask any doctor worth their salt for the story of how it is to watch someone die.

Have them describe to you the cutting of the power line somewhere inside the skull, the cessation of electric currents in the region. The veil being drawn over the statue. Water draining away.

You can lose the final breath if you fail to pay attention. Red to black.

Remember all their names. Keep a list. Say them out loud to yourself.

ACTIVE LISTENING

You say the first consultation is free. I say
I am fully aware of the nature of this transaction.
Let me ease your way, Doctor, and preempt—
or is it paraphrase—your explanations. You want
me to talk about my brother. I want to play a game.
You know the rules: here are my words, tossed
across the room for you to receive, reconfigure,
and return. Parrot back as question: *Is this
the thing you feel?* You tell me what its name is.
I know this is your way of proving to yourself
and to myself what you have heard—*I am confirming
understanding. I hear the you that you are speaking. I am here.*
As if to say it takes years to train the ear to scalpel-
sharpness. As if to say it only takes ninety minutes
in your pastel-colored office to know this girl
down to her smallest sounds: ductile strands
of muscle snapping taut. Cross, uncross the arms,
square the shoulders high in fighting stance, guard
the heart, cover the jugular, drive steel into the spine.
Say it like this: *Your nails are bitten down to the quick,
my dear. Have you had a good cry about this?* Now take
some more questions: What is a good cry? Where is
my brother? Now take an honest answer: the morning
I was born, all my crying had to be struck from me.
My brother is the crier. Listen: here is something
that passes for a joke. Now laugh.

THE LAW OF IMPENETRABILITY

A quality of matter: no two bodies can occupy the same space at the same time.

We can experiment around this hypothesis. If A drops a stone into a full cup of water, the stone will displace the water. If A drops an egg from the kitchen counter, it will blow apart when it hits the floor. If A is in a speeding car and does not see the turn ahead, does not mark the taillights of B's van around the bend, does not push her right foot fast enough against the brakes, then— If A stands beside B, lies on top of B, sits on B's lap, then—

If A and B are two bodies in the closest possible proximity, then at least one of the two will mistake *close* for *whole.* Possibly both will make this mistake, will imagine breaking themselves down to the same subatomic particle. They will think they have found themselves one there. The desire to believe this is a natural compulsion, instinctive as breath

but I know for a fact that bodies would get between. All matter is impenetrable by law. There is no cure for lonely, no more opaque surface than flesh, no sites for *connect* but *collide, emergency, there's been an accident—*

In light of this law, record your findings. The water spills and we pick particles of eggshell from the splattered slime. Around the bend, two cars crumple. A and B break against each other, the impact itself proof

there is a rational explanation for everything. This is mine, for why you may not touch me.

AN INVENTORY

Only this: the ward, the bed, and you
and the hours at which the food
appears by your door—eight
twelve four eight according to the body's need.
The boys in the scrubs going soft-footed
through the ward, hands gloved in latex
to keep the offerings pure. Plastic tray.
Palm-sized mound of rice caged in cling wrap.
Lukewarm slab of pale anemic flesh that would be
chicken if you believed in the cycle of rebirth—
something now only the possibility of chicken
with a side of carrots, symmetrically cubed. Salt content
minimal. Sufficient nutritional value to sustain life.

Any life. Your life in this body that closes
and opens its eyes on the same room
every day. With each meal the same invocation
by the same petitioners echoing, a frequency
only we can perceive. *Will you eat today?*
Will you speak to us? Tell us what is
wrong slipped sideways under the noise.
Steel tray on counter clattering. Plastic plates
and forks and spoons, all edges worn down
so dull they cut only food. Your flesh is safe now.
You can feed yourself without pain.

OBJECT PERMANENCE

The hardest lesson to teach a child is about the axis
on which the universe spins. When you're young
you hold the world at arm's length. From ages zero to x,
we fix ourselves in the inevitable center, the only place
from which we need not be afraid of missing something.
Mom, I'll tell you now that this is the first difficult
conversation we will ever have. You wonder why
it feels as though you're playing peek-a-boo with a wall,
why the baby doesn't laugh. I hate this game. I always have,
because it's a magic trick I can't see inside of, no more
than you can read the signs in my head. The question
of your existence is too grave to tickle my funny bone.
When I take the steel balls of my fists to your arms,
remember this is the only way my youngest self
knows how to love, always half-terrified of things
it can't see. Put down your hands so I can remember
what you look like, relearn the shape of your nose.
Convince me your eyes haven't transformed,
suddenly, into the most lightless of black holes—
that since I can observe you, you must still be here.

THE LAW OF GRAVITY

Today I learned that gravity is an invisible force
that draws objects toward each other. As in,
the planets toward the sun. As in, a *me* toward
a *you* in a love song where the principle of the thing
holds, even if the science is dubious. As in, a child
toward the far wall of a room, on stumpy legs
making it up as they go along, step by step, bone
by newly hardened bone. As in, a mother toward
that child, hands outstretched but never touching
certainly never holding, only ever murmuring
go slowly now, slowly—where the spirit of words
holds even if the child has no language yet,
or so she hopes.

Today I learned that gravity is the force by which
a planet or other body draws objects toward its center.
Today I am the child who learns that when she falls
and tears her knee open on the ground, and sees
the pain bright red inside herself for the first time—
that, my girl, is only the pull of the earth. As in, only
the earth wanting to pull you close. As in, only the earth
doing what mothers do. And when my own mother
comes and does not draw me to her, but instead kneels
to see me eye to eye and tells me this pain is nothing
to be broken up about because it has not shattered me
that is when I know I can stand again, bleeding knee
and dirty palms, without help.

Today I learned that Earth's gravity is what keeps you
on the ground and what makes things fall. Ask any child
what gravity does and they'll say it makes things fall. As in,
the cup from the tabletop. As in, the garbage can headfirst
like a body hitting the ground when you kick it over to reveal
more bottles, more broken glass, more things nobody wants
that may pierce you if you don't know careful like I do. As in,
let the child fall so she learns what will and will not break her.
As in, let the child fall so she learns not to be a fragile thing.
Knock her around all you like. It'll give her an edge.

LA NIÑA

You've never claimed to know
what it all means, why women
and why names, if the naming
is to soften or to warn, but
things of the sky are not for you
to question. There is no disaster
in this city, where the rain
wears a girl's face and we call
her as we call our sisters.
The storms that batter us
are sisters all. Look out
the window and imagine
them—sunless skin, long
spidering hands, curtain
of black hair tangling
and untangling. No one will
tell you they see different
in this city. Here we traffic
in the allegorical, thigh-deep
in the gutter-water tide. The rain
is sister, and she demands
you look up. Open your mouth.
Learn to sing your resilience
as the gutters overflow. Smile
for the five o'clock news. Keep
singing; do not ever stop.

LAZARUS JEWEL BOX

something not to tell the children
when you go barefoot together
across the hot sand:

dig deep with your hands
into the foam where
the water breaks itself

after the sea has dispensed
with its dead, we come
sun in our eyes
to collect the coffins

THE LAW OF CONSERVATION

Today I cremated my cousin.
I come now to tell you what it was like.

All the members of my extended family lined up
in single file before the casket, to look at her face
one final time. I suppose to say goodbye.
Then they—I don't know who—wheeled it

into the furnace. What came out an hour later
could fit in a silver jar, in the cradle
of one arm—skin, bone, hair, and ashes.

Just the one jar. Not so difficult to imagine. She
had always been a small girl. Nothing comes from
nothing, and nothing passes away. Matter and energy
can neither be created nor destroyed, only transfigured
and rearranged within closed systems. That's the rule.

No obscure knowledge, just grade-school science
textbook stuff. So elementary I still remember
all the figures it has led to: *When we die, our bodies
become the grass, and the antelope eat the grass.*

Or, something more celestial: *we are all made of stars.*
Every molecule of carbon in the body a memento
from another life. Every moment you respire,
the privilege of remembering: life is a circle, no

such thing as waste, the moral of the story is
we need not even be celestial to achieve
transfiguration. Everything is more beautiful
when compared to the stars, in the end.
The moral of the story is you only grieve
because you do not understand. Or, you grieve
because these things are not for you to understand.
Or: because I did not know better, one aunt held me
without my asking and said my grieving was forgiven.

That must be what strangers on the internet now mean
when they tell me I want a physicist to speak at my funeral.
I will never see her again, and yet her existence persists
and is conserved. The principle of the thing is forever.
Why split hairs about form?

GOD NEVER BLINKS

Here are your results.
Your body is no temple.

Look instead at how
the cancer has bloomed
pinkly into a forest
wedged roots down the holes
in your bones.

Fireproofed
against any medical
procedure—too late
but look how absolute
the devastation.

This is the secret we
uncover in none
of those white rooms
where doctors convince us
the machines see everything

though they have no hands
to lay on us no mouths
to whisper your sins
are forgiven stand up
and live. Every created thing

can forget its own death.
This gift alone is proof
there is a God
and that He loves us.

IN STATU VIATORIS

Thesis 1: Hope is when the soul is in darkness and turns toward a light that it cannot yet perceive.

Here we understand the soul as the self, the subject, the "I," and darkness as a state of trial, for instance, captivity, powerlessness, loss, or solitude. Marcel uses the act of "turning toward" to describe an orientation of openness, a yearning to be delivered from the trial that is the obverse side of total despair. Despair obscures any possibilities of a different future, as the present conditions appear to the despairing person as permanently frozen. This can lead to a sense of desperation and eventually a giving up, and the despairing person often withdraws from life into isolation and alienation from others. But Marcel argues that only when the temptation to despair is present can hope emerge—in this sense, hope is a returning home, a means of finding one's own way, of coming back to the meaning and value of one's life.

II

EATING DISORDER NOT OTHERWISE SPECIFIED

Answer the following questions with YES or NO. Are you a perfectionist, a person who always wants to be in control, an overachiever? Do you scrutinize yourself over small faults? Do you have a hard time saying no? Do you think you are not good enough, stupid, or worthless? Do you often find yourself comparing yourself to others? Are you taking this test in public, where others can see the computer screen?

What do these questions have to do with missing breakfast in the morning?

*

The doctor asks do I have
a habit of cutting
my food into small pieces.
I tell him it is an art, the same
as sculpture, poetry,
folding paper into cranes
or flowers or other,
more beautiful shapes.

*

My mother tells me no,
sweetheart, I am beautiful.

*

I remember the last time someone
pinched my cheeks—a cousin's
husband's sister's friend's great-aunt.
She called them *baby fat*, said
it was charming to still find me
so soft. I laughed, and put my fork
through her hand in my mind.

*

My lola's been praying for my soul
for as long as I can remember.
Sometimes I'm a little girl
again, being told Finish
your food, think of the children
starving in Africa. Open your eyes
to how blessed you are.
Swallow it whole.
Choke on it.

*

Let me tell you what I've read about sickness.

How much I weigh in actuality means nothing next to what the mirrors show me. My distorted self-image is the result of various cognitive biases that alter how I, an affected individual, evaluate and think about my body, food, and eating. I may

practice repetitive weighing, measuring, and mirror-gazing.
This is a common practice, known as "body checking."

Tell me things I don't know.

*

The doctor tells me there is a name
for people like me. I tell the doctor
this must be worth more words
than some Latin on an index card.

*

In 1994, Kevin Carter won the Pulitzer Prize
for photographing hunger. His camera gave it
wings and the head of a vulture.

Photojournalists were not allowed
to touch famine victims, for fear
of spreading disease. Look at the children
starving a continent away. You are blessed.
Be ashamed of the meat on your bones.
That same year he killed himself.

These are things I know because I've read them.

*

What is the language of sickness?
In English, please.
Do they not teach you
to idiot-proof your speech in
medical school? Tell the truth.
If your doctor isn't lying to you,
what obscures his penmanship?

*

My lola
tells me in her day,
hija, girls
were like flowers.
I'm a girl today.
What are girls like
today? When did they stop
being flowers?

*

If you were another person,
would you be friends with you?
Every morning I inspect myself
naked in the mirror. I am waiting
for the "yes" to emerge from the glass.

*

Lola, instead of talking,
pack all my meals
into airtight tupperwares.
Send them to Africa,
because those starving children
will take you to heaven.

*

I am told I'm not
like one of those girls.

ANAPHYLAXIS

      tells you these symptoms
are your body fighting
to protect itself what burns
through your blood is desire

on hyperdrive tightening
airways squeezing your breath
in its fists there are

no safe words
only the needle

shot of epinephrine clear
liquid a messenger here

are your orders stand
down stand down
stand down

      tells you name
the enemy which
foods which drugs
which insect bites

    tells you watch what you put
in your mouth tells you a walk
in the park like a dance

through a minefield there
are things with wings fire
coming fire between
the flowers fire

    will not tell you
the truth sometimes is
only malfunction

your body hates you and wants you dead

why else this war these
fictional poisons why else
this pretend naming
what is unwelcome

sometimes there is no known cause

METASTASIS

Here are your results.

Love, the doctor says
the bougainvillea
are growing wild again.

The vines overrun
your balcony. They spill
over every last stone
in your wall. Even now,

as we speak in this
pale barren room,
they are putting down
roots in the concrete.

You are turning, love,
into a flowering tree.
Who would have guessed
that the chronic pain

you've complained of
these three months past
would turn out to be
a real thorn in your side.

Now we can sit and see it clear
how overgrown everything inside
you has become—another thorn
and another, and another

every vertebra waiting
to burst into bloom.

PARASOMNIA

if you do not know what the sound is
here is a list of things you might
compare it to fireworks gunshot backfiring
engine thunder accompanied by flashes
of light cymbals door slamming shut heavy
footsteps something coming for you

the thing is most often there is no dream
or at least none you can remember
no story to ascribe to the sound no images
except a light your gut knows not to follow
sometimes a muscle spasm as when your body
remembers it was once a hunted thing
that started at loud noises coiled and tensed
at once to bolt or to fall on them snarling

although its name is very vivid exploding
head syndrome should not cause
you pain at most confusion at most fear at most
a terror you will soon rise from eyes open
cognizant there is no real cause for alarm
now you are awake you need only be awake

HYPERVIGILANCE

take a deep breath and name

five things you can see

the empty bed
the empty bed
whitewash
wet floor
the empty bed

four things you can touch

wet floor wooden
door kitchen table's edge
telephone ringing

three things you can
hear telephone ringing
sirens open water

two things you can
smell iron in the water (take
a deep breath) the water
still running one thing
one thing you can taste

the inside of my
mouth the inside of
my mouth the inside
of my mouth

IN STATU VIATORIS

Thesis 2: Hope is a response of positive non-acceptance to a situation of captivity in which my soul finds itself.

And just like that it is as though no time has passed at all, and I am at the university again, reading the continental philosophers. One dead French man says that we live our lives in pursuit of our one precious thing, something that is forever lost and forever desired. Here we see that desire is not characterized by objects but by absence. You only realize the thing you have lost by examining the shape of the space it left behind. Meanwhile, another dead French man says that to love a being means to affirm that they shall not die. This is supposedly the greatest hope there is. Who is the lover if not someone who believes in the ability of the beloved to survive death? Who is the lover if not someone who lives in paradoxes—who is able to say, with unbearable certainty, I will see you again soon, I'll see you when I do, anytime, any place that is?

A MIRACLE STORY

More healing stories are told about Jesus than any other figure in the Jewish tradition. The earliest sources contain widespread attestation to Jesus' healings—on historical grounds, it is near indisputable that Jesus was a healer and an exorcist.

The Gospel narratives in which Jesus heals are classified form-critically as Miracle Stories. Typically, a Miracle Story begins with a description of the situation, followed by a miracle, the results confirming the miracle, and the response of the onlookers.

Let the sick man call upon the priests of the church, let them pray over him, anointing him with oil in the name of the Lord. The prayer of faith shall save the sick man. Brothers and sisters, we believe in faith.

Lord, I am not worthy to have you come under my roof, but only say the word and my soul shall be healed. Lord, I am not worthy to receive you, but only say the word and I shall be healed. Lord, if you wish it, you can make me well.

Jesus' healing ministry would have been interpreted as healing by means of divine power. Additionally, there is a dimension to it that sets him apart from other purportedly divine healers, both Jewish and pagan—Jesus' eschatological interpretation of his healing activity. Jesus understands the healings that he performs as signs of the Kingdom of God.

*Come to me, all you
who are weary
and burdened,
and I will give you rest.
Take my yoke upon you
and learn from me
for I am meek
and humble of heart.*

It must be stressed that, different from all other known examples, Jesus healed all who were brought to him, not simply one or two individuals at different times. Jesus' ability to heal universally would have commended him to the masses as an extraordinary individual.

*Then a man
named Jairus
came and fell
at the feet of Jesus.
My little girl
is dying, will you come
and put your hands on her
that she might live?*

In many instances, as in the healing of the daughter of Jairus, there can be found references to the fact that Jesus required faith as a prerequisite in order to heal. Conversely, it is said explicitly that Jesus, upon his return to Nazareth, was only able to heal a few people because of their general unbelief.

Critical historians tend to assess Jesus' healings in the Gospels either as legendary accretions to the narrative of Jesus' life, or as the purely natural curing of psychosomatic maladies. Often behind such assumptions is the presupposition that it is impossible to attribute such healings to the direct intervention of God into the world. In their view the historical Jesus did not perform anything miraculous.

*While Jesus
was speaking,
someone came
from the house
of Jairus.
Your daughter
is dead. She
has closed her eyes
and gone quiet
as breath
into the long sleep.
Do not bother
the master
anymore.*

*That little girl
is not dead,
she is only sleeping.
Wake up, little girl.*

SHOOT THE MESSENGER

Open with a greeting.

> Hello. Good morning/afternoon/evening.

Identify yourself; ask the identity of the person you are talking to and their relationship to the patient.

> This is ____, a resident at ____ Hospital. I am currently on the health-care team for ____. May I know who I am speaking to, please, and how you are related to the patient?

Ask to speak to the person closest to the patient (ideally, the health-care proxy or the contact person indicated in the chart). Avoid responding to any direct question until you have verified the identity of the person to whom you are speaking.

> May I please speak with ____?

> I'm sorry, I'm not at liberty to answer that. May I please speak with ____?

> May I please speak with ____?

Ask if the contact person is alone. If you don't have a prior relationship with the person you are speaking to, ask what they know about the patient's condition.

> Hello,   . How are you? Are you alone at the moment?

Fire a warning shot.

> I'm afraid I have some bad news.

Use clear and direct language, no medical jargon. Euphemisms like "expired," "passed away," or "didn't make it" must be avoided, as these can be misinterpreted. Instead, words such as "dead" or "died" should be used and repeated several times.

> I'm sorry,   .   has died.

Speak clearly and slowly, allow time for questions; be empathetic. Be prepared to facilitate the grief reaction where necessary. A perceptive listener can easily tell whether the notifier cares about the patient and their family members or is merely going through the motions.

> I'm sorry for your loss. This must be so difficult for you.

If you feel uncomfortable about delivering the death notification via telephone, please ask for help from your supervisor. If necessary, you may pass the task on to a colleague with more experience.

ACTIVE LISTENING

I say I am telling you what I saw—
the bathroom door rolling back
like a stone from the tomb's mouth,
how the hole yawned, released my brother
back up into the light. I say I can show you
where his hair had dripped
a small flood across the hallway floor.
I saw the cross-hatching on his wrists,
red lines I knew like the letters of my name.
You ask what happened next and I say
my father wrote the numbers on my hand for
the ambulance; I sat through the hundred rings.
I breathed *Hello* into the phone. *Hello*
and the water took all the other words from me.
My brother and I were alone
but I was not all there. Not at all there.
You say again *Tell me—*
I say there is no what else.

I say there is no what else.
You say again *Tell me—*
but I was not all there. Not at all there.
My brother and I were alone
and the water took my words from me.
I breathed *Hello* into the phone. *Hello.*
The ambulance. I sat through the hundred rings
my father wrote the numbers on my hand for.
You ask what happened next and I say
red lines I knew like the letters of my name.
I saw the cross-hatching on his wrists,
a small flood across the hallway floor
where his hair had dripped.
I say, *I can show you. Back up into the light.*
How the hole yawned, released my brother
like a stone from the tomb's mouth.
The bathroom door rolling back.
I say I am telling you what I saw.

I say there is no what else.

ALL THINGS BRIGHT AND BEAUTIFUL

This is the White City.

This is the tower
at the heart of the White City.

This is the tree
that stands in the tower
at the heart of the White City.

These are the needles
of the silver tree
at rest in the tower
at the heart of the White City.

This is the girl
fed by the needles
that sprout from the tree
upright in the tower
at the heart of the White City.

This is a lace dress for the doll
in the lap of the girl
who watches the needles
like vines on the tree
on guard in the tower
at the heart of the White City.

These are the flowers that cover the walls
and bloom in the lace on the skirts of the dolls
embraced by the girl
drinking from needles
hanging down from the tree
that rules in the tower
at the heart of the White City.

These are the faces of Father and Mother
pale as the flowers infesting the walls.
This is the cracked china flesh of the dolls
tucked next to the girl
whose hands are all needles
from the iron tree
that grows in the tower
at the heart of the White City.

This is a prayer to love one another
as dust in the mouths of her father and mother,
pressed flat as the flowers that paper the walls.
These are the hands that dress the dolls
for the sleeping girl
pierced through with needles
creeping down from the tree
alive in the tower
at the heart of the White City.

These are the angels that stand by the door
who write the prescription—*Love one another*—
and slide it across toward Father and Mother.
These are the flowers they peel from the walls.
This is the dust that collects on the dolls
on the bed of the girl
who clutched at the needles
that fell from the tree
steadfast in the tower
at the heart of the White City.

This is the paper and ink on the floor
at the feet of the angels who stand at the door
and study for years how to love one another
as love has dismantled the father and mother
painting new flowers to life on the walls,
assembling brown boxes as homes for the dolls
by the bed of the girl
silver as the needles
at the foot of the tree
that bloomed in the tower
at the heart of the White City.

These are the bills and the tests and the score
crumpled, collecting in hills on the floor
kicked up by the angels who walk to the door
and spell out the order to love one another
in rosary beads strung for Father and Mother.
These are the flowers that cracked through the walls,
flowers at rest in the hands of the dolls
that belonged to the girl
who lived on the needles
of the iron tree
alone in the tower
at the heart of the White City.

III

IN STATU VIATORIS

Thesis 3: Hope must undergo purification—from the specific and limited "I hope that" to "I hope," "I hope in," and finally, "I hope in Thee for us."

Today I have to focus on piecing all these things together. So close is the bond we establish between love and suffering in our experience that we have come to think of suffering accepted with joy as the most authentic sign of love with any depth at all. I was taught this is the line between pain and purity, and that walking that line is how you save not only yourself but the one you love, the one for whom you suffer, the one who is worth all your suffering. If you test me on all this I will know you want me to smile and, like a thing with feathers, open my mouth and sing the songs I was taught to sing, but it is one thing to know and another to believe. I am aware of the paradox that is dead white men coming back to tell me what I should hope for, and in whom, but not why. I know what the rhetoric of hope is worth. I am prepared to fail this test.

TODAY WE ARE CANCELING THE APOCALYPSE

for May, my co-pilot; after Guillermo del Toro

So I saw that movie, my father told me one day, *and it was fun but it's funny that you like it so much.* And I knew
which parts he meant were funny ha-ha versus
funny strange, just as it was equal parts ha-ha

and strange to imagine him squinting at his iPad
in the dark after work, wondering about this monster film
where the end of the world comes from beneath the sea
and humankind deploys giant robots to kill it

as soon as it breaks the surface. My father watched
to see what two hours of things smashing
other things had to say about his poem-writing daughter
his soft-talking daughter, his daughter

whose violence is all in her silences, his daughter
whose favorite movie should conceivably be,
what do you call it, something more cerebral.
Everyone wonders this about me, when they know.

The first order of business before the battle starts: name your enemy. It goes something like this:

The kaiju sighted at 1700 hours on the first of May 2021 breaks the surface of the Sea of Japan off the coast of Dalnegorsk, making for the shore. The image on the monitors is broad and bipedal, with a curved horn crowning the top of its head and two axelike spikes of bone protruding from its back. Armored all over except at the joints and the base of the throat, where the plates taper down into bare flesh. The pilots studying this image have already closed in on those points—discerning places to strike, how to reach them with greatest efficiency. Simulation start. Target: Category 4 kaiju. Codename: Hookheart.

Say it like this: breach date 10 June 2021. Category 3 kaiju codename Rusalka, sighted at 0400 hours. Agile, serpentine body. Light dorsal armor offset by superior speed quotient. Jagged claws and tail-pincer. Highly toxic. This one is not a simulation, but you have trained against enough computer-generated images to survive this encounter. Perhaps even the ones that come after.

There will always be the ones that come after. If you can name them, you will know how to kill them when they arrive. Restart the clock.

Except the thing is the monsters are not the scary part.
At least not to me. This is where I tell you the scary part

a little before it comes, when we are watching together
our eyes full of the lights of a city that will be destroyed

two scenes from now: the truth is the monsters are nothing.
Everything terrifying about this story is in the Drift

even if, cinematically, it's only twenty seconds or so
of fast cuts through a character's childhood, through

their life desaturated and filtered over with blue—
nothing more than having another person in your head

and suddenly seeing all the pieces no one else gets
to observe, knowing they are looking at you

and you have nowhere to hide, knowing that
is how you are expected to save the world.

You already know what's coming, but this is what it's all about:
The girl stands with her partner in the head of the machine.
Together they try to make it move, and then to make it fight.
The girl chases a rabbit even if she has been told not to,
into a city that stands whole only in memory. She comes
out into memory on the last day that it is ever whole.
The girl in memory is small and unarmored. She wears only
a blue coat, carries in hand a red shoe with a broken strap.
The girl sees the monster destroy the city purely by accident
for no reason other than that she had been visiting the city
when it emerged from the sea. The girl has lost her family
in the crowd and cannot find them. The girl has lost her
family under the rubble and will never find them again.
Now, here in the ashes the girl walks to see the quiet
that has devoured everything. The girl does not remember
she has already lived through this. The girl has lost her way
in the things she remembers. The girl does not remember

there are other battles now that need her attention. The girl does not remember she was never meant to do battle alone. The girl is a woman with human blood red on her hands and monster blood running blue in her hair.

The girl is already a soldier. The girl is only a girl.

Here is something no one will tell you
only because it's not exciting enough
on the surface to put on a movie poster:

All of us are looking in the wrong direction.
The real battles are in your head long
before you take them to the water.

Maybe this is the only reason
that matters: that I like imagining
the world ending in water

that I like imagining
what I would go to war for
in the end.

the truth is I'm wondering who

it will be that finally tells me

there at the end that I will not

face down the apocalypse alone

and who will stand beside me

shoulder to shoulder as the sea

swells to swallow everything

the monsters have not destroyed

and who will I look to and who

will I vow to for once without fear

of making promises I will prove

not strong enough to see through

that should anything still living seek

to cut you from the heart of this

machine they will have to tear me

from you first they will have

to tear me from you first

And this is the part where
I tell you the ending
as a reward for having come
this far with me:

even after the girl comes up
from the seafloor, and her partner
starts to breathe again, and the blue sky
goes black with chopper birds come
to carry their spent soldiers home

even after the marshal says to stop
the clock, and a thousand human voices
shout that the war is over, and the ocean shines
as though to say you're safe now, no one

will die here anymore—
others will come after. Others
will always come after, and we

will rise to meet them, again
and again and again.

ACTIVE LISTENING

You say, *we haven't heard from you. What are your thoughts?*
I say, well, Doc, I'm not sure what you want me to say.

That's a truthful thought. That's one you got out of me. Next.
You say, *you've been quiet all this time. How do you feel now?*

Right now? And I say now? Right now? Right now I am feeling
an ache in my back. Dull, localized between the scapula.

A four out of ten if you would like me to rate my pain. A little
like how I imagine growing wings feels, if you would like

a pretty metaphor on the side of that. That counts, doesn't it,
for something I'm feeling? Was that what you wanted
   to know?

Are you going to tell me to lower my shoulders because I hold
   them
like a boxer, because your educated gaze can identify the fifty ways

I'm strung tight, sitting across you in this beautiful white office
with flowers on the table, not telling you what you expect
   to hear?

Ask why I curl my hands in like flowers yet to bloom, open
   them only
to curl them tighter, until my knuckles are all bare bone no flesh

to speak of, and my palms would have little moons dug in them
if I wasn't the sort of person to bite my nails down. Tell me
  the sort

of person I am. I know that's what they're paying you to do.
You say, *you look like a girl who needs to lose it for a while* and I ask

lose it like my brother almost lost it? Lose it like we almost
  lost him,
like we didn't just cut it deadly close? I ask, so this is all just
  data, then? I ask

do you have a file in one of your desk drawers for girls like me?
  Is there
a word for us, the sort of word you'd use in an academic study,
  the sort

of study that gets you gigs at conferences where everyone wears
  spotless white
and speaks the same spotless language, and knows exactly what
  you mean

when you say *girls like her. Kids like that.* I fucking know what
  words are, Doc.
I deal in them the same as you. When you smash them against a
  solid surface

you'll get a cutting thing, all edges, no way to hold it that
  doesn't also
bleed you from the places you touch. No apologies. I'm sorry,
  you did ask

what I was thinking. Am I losing it to your satisfaction, Doc?
   Do you want
more clichés about things that shatter? Do you want to break
   me open

with your questions and take credit for every vein of gold you
   use to join
the sundered pieces? I know the metaphors you use for this;
   I know

how scar tissue forms thick and armor-like over skin and that's
   what passes
for growing strong, what builds character, what raises chances
   of survival

as if survival's the only name of this game. As if all that matters
   is I'm alive now
to be a good story, the kind someone else can learn from, right?
   As if my brother

is sleeping soundly today and I'm here in your office to tell you
   everything
turned out all right in the end after all. Right, Doc? I'm
   supposed to say it's all right

so that when you're finally through with studying me you can
   have the last word,
turn me over to my family and say, here, here's your beauty of an
   eldest daughter.

Look how she glitters now, and forget how we let her fall.

BREAKING NEWS

Life at sea begins by chance.
Ferry passengers assured of safe
and pleasant experience. Captain
said to have spent four decades
at sea. Colleague describes Captain
as nicest person on ship. Captain
speaks with poetic flair about the reds
of sunset and sunrise. Captain
appears on television dressed in white
uniform with gold epaulettes on shoulders.
Crew members interviewed know
little about Captain's personal life. Captain
is paraded before cameras, face hidden
in shadow cast by hood of windbreaker.
Captain crashed into a door on the bridge
but sustained only light injuries according
to onshore doctor. Captain decides to delay
evacuation. Interview transcript shows ship's crew
worried about lack of rescue boats for passengers.
Captain and crew take to rescue boats before
passengers. All of surviving crew face charges
of negligence and abandoning passengers.
The conduct of captain and crew declared
unfathomable from the viewpoint of common
sense, unsupportable, tantamount to murder.

Captain has not explained why he left the vessel.
Captain feared passengers being swept away
by ferocious currents if they leapt into the sea.
Trouserless captain of sinking ferry scrambles
to safety as hundreds remain trapped inside.
Captain runs out of ship without his pants on.

AS THE STORYTELLER
after Richard Siken

I'll tell you about the day we spent folding paper cranes
                           and the air picked them up in its hands
      and flew them. How we live in a city with two suns,
    where children
               pray to wake the wind. Only then do the birds
remember what the bones in their wings were created hollow for.
          To walk through the city is to forget
                about finding somewhere to end, is the gift
              of as many lives
    as there are people on the road, as there are
               lampposts to see corners by. One day I'll take you
walking. Your mornings will be pink and orange, every minute
                                a sickle moon.
Don't look out the window if you want the day to keep its color.
This means
       I'm bargaining with the night for your time, this
       means evenings
           locked in battle. I'll give you something to stay for,
    tell you I've counted all our days for a certainty.
               I'll tell you our bodies are two suns,
                     and it's stories that rescue our light.

SCATTERING

My brother is made of light.
I have known this since he was big enough

to run, since I was old enough to fear
for what I'd find beneath his skin

should he fall and scrape a knee.
My brother looks to his older sister

for a knowledge that stands against
all his questions. He is young enough

driven by nothing heavier
than a hunger for the world.

Why are the sea and the sky blue
are there more colors than the eye

refracts back to us, how light are birds
that the tides of air can lift them

how did the universe begin. It doesn't matter
that I can't straighten the science, only that I speak

with measurable certainty. Light is so delicate
it hits the air and scatters into its component colors.

A clear cloudless day-time sky is blue
because molecules in the air scatter

more blue light from the sun than red.
When we look at sunset, we see red

and orange because the blue has scattered
out and away from the line of sight.

But I don't how old my brother is
when he discovers what he is made of.

It slips out of him, a confession, one night
in the living room, over a bowl of chips

a video game we fight together on. His fingers tap
square, square, triangle. Onscreen the lady of war

aims a kick, legs like willow branches
roundhousing down a line of foot soldiers.

They are computer-generated identical.
They dissolve bloodlessly against the ground

too digital to stain her shoes. She wears a purple
silk sheath dress and a golden phoenix in her hair

and it is half-crown and half-statue
and the dust of battle does not settle on it.

We're awake. At 3 a.m., these virtual bodies feel firmer
than the ones we sit in, crunching at potato chips

to make sound happen. My brother asks me why
must I inhabit this body. Why am I not winged

and rising hollow-boned into the scattering blue
and am I so hollow the air will scatter me.

I do not tell him it cannot be verified.
I have no way to logic him out of his body

and into the princess, to overwrite his long arms
with wings. I don't say we aren't digital anymore.

This isn't the kingdom of our video games
where winning wars is a matter of hand-eye

coordination, depth perception, precise pushes
of buttons—where we can stand an army of one

against a thousand generics, where phoenixes nest
in our hair. I do not tell him I have no knowledge

to armor you with, no quicksilver insight
into how we might learn to own ourselves.

What I have for you are measurements—mass
and density, figures to mark the human form as

too heavy for the sky. You would need oceans of it
to break against. You would need wings for miles.

SURGERY

I ask you what you're learning at school.
You say nothing new, only that the books
reaffirm the oldest knowledges there are—

    that steady hands can save a life.

I imagine you lifting the hood
of a stalled car, taking scalpel to flesh,
finding it's

        machinery
        that beats inside us.

There are few more certain things
than an inventory of parts. Like this:

four chambers in the heart, three
major arteries, twenty-seven bones

in hand and wrist, each
with its own name. Excise all
that does not belong. Run the fluids
up the right pipes, and await breath.
Assume all that breathes is also alive.

And here is the form of my agreement:

    There are few things more solid
    than hands you squeeze

        so hard the bones come together,
        twenty-seven points of contact
        clicking beneath skin. The sound
        signals something is still here, where

        here
        is inside the machine.

The girl

    who bites her fingernails,
    twiddles her thumbs
    in a questioning
    circle, will never turn the pages
    of an anatomy book,

is asking you
to find out what it is.
If your books have anything

        to say about

            what animates the bones
            in those hands, what speaks
            them into life—

look for me. Tell me the answer.

PAGPAG

With the dead, we are taught
always to say no. Bury your dead
barefoot to keep their steps
from your door. Break the rosary
you place in their hands. Do not say
thank you to condolences or goodbye
when guests leave the chapel.
Do not walk them to the exit
while the candles are still burning.
Do not sleep. Do not bring the dust,
the dirt, the dead off the road
into your house. Take the long way.
Walk in a spiral toward a center
you cannot see. Have faith.
When you make it home, change
your clothes immediately. You want
them back, but not like this. Don't wait.

TRUE FACTS ABOUT THE SEA TURTLE

Chelonia *is based on the Greek word* kelone, *for armour.*
—Barbara Brennessel

The meaning of the word *memory* differs from region to region.
The exact ancestry of memories has been disputed.

Memories are characterized by a special bony
or cartilaginous shell, which acts as a shield.
The memory cannot crawl out of its shell.

The shape of the shell gives helpful clues about how a memory
lives. Land memories are famous for moving slowly
in part because of their heavy, cumbersome shells.
Amphibious memories often have webbed feet and long claws.
Sea memories fly through the water.

Memories lay eggs that are slightly soft and leathery.
Large numbers of eggs are deposited in holes
dug into mud or sand. They are then covered
and left to incubate by themselves.
When the memories hatch, they squirm their way
to the surface and head toward water.
Immature memories are not cared for by adults.

Although many memories spend much of their lives underwater, all memories breathe air and must surface at regular intervals. Memories breathe in two ways.

Memories are social creatures and sometimes switch between monogamy and promiscuity in their sexual behavior. Case studies also exist of memories that have enjoyed playing.

The flesh of memories was, and still is, considered a delicacy in a number of cultures. Wild memories continue to be caught and sent to market in large numbers.

THE HEART OF THE BLUE WHALE

My sister dreams of seeing a blue whale
in the wild one day. She says she loves them
for how big they are, blood vessels like tunnels
hearts heavy as cars. She's driving right now
as she tells me to imagine the crawl through
the arteries to reach this heart. Imagine listening
to the whale's bloodstream and hearing the roll
of the ocean, one journey within and one
without. Imagine all the singing they must do
on the sea's roads, a tune for every current
reverberating up from depths so crushing
only machines can follow. I plug the aux cord in
and say I hear the whales anytime we sing together
in her car at dusk, leaving the university behind us
for home. When I play "Love on the Weekend"
on Fridays, because sometimes that's enough to feel
you've made it somewhere. When John says
I'll be the DJ, she'll be the driver, like he can see
me and this tiny person and the fearless way
she brings her seat right up to the wheel. He strums.
I say there's no ocean in this song, and we live now
in the smack middle of a dehydrated city, but maybe
these drives we take are the same—some kind
of migratory pattern, one way of knowing the world
that happens in the blood. Who can say, really

how anything knows where to go? All we know
is when we're on the highway we hear the tide
that will take us where we belong, and what carries us
is no less than a heart made of steel and gasoline
and the thrum of a stranger's guitar
and her little voice, and mine.

ORIGIN STORIES

1.

Noun.
The cessation of all bodily functions
necessary to sustain life. Causes
include biological aging, predation,
malnutrition, disease, homicide,
starvation, dehydration, accidents,
trauma, terminal injury. Bodies
of living organisms begin
to decompose shortly after. Commonly
considered a sad, unpleasant,
or fearful occasion.

2.

Stoppage of heartbeat, pulse,
and breathing. Most organs—the eye,
the kidney—remain alive,
and can be used for transplantation.

3.

The degeneration of tissue
in the brain, followed by
the failure of most organs. These
cannot be used for transplantation.
Rigor has set in.

4.

And the Lord said unto Moses,
Tell your people to mark the blood
of a lamb above their doors, and I,
seeing the blood, will pass over you,
and not suffer the destroyer to enter.

5.

Death came airborne into the world
when lightning first cracked open
the egg of the sky, spilling
an oily black rain of snakes.

6.

The end of the world is hidden
in a triangle of ocean, into which
entire cities have disappeared.

7.

No one knows the name
of the fruit anymore, but rarely someone
will have dreams of its sweetness, of the garden,
and the swords of angels.

8.

In some mythologies, the first thing
to die is a man with an infant son
in his arms dancing backward into the sea,
is a king's beautiful daughter, is the youngest
and most beloved of the ancient gods.

9.

A boy in striped pajamas.
A robed skeleton on horseback
who speaks in capitals, drinks tea,
adopts daughter, names a son-in-law,
gives his manservant Sundays off.
A smiling girl with a black umbrella.
Brad Pitt. David Bowie. Your boyfriend.
Anyone who wears a human face,
goes by a nickname, speaks.

10.

The Lord said, I have already saved
the good, all those who never truly
belonged down here. What will we do
now? It will come to us.

11.

In the oldest days of the world
Bathala could chase Death
down to the point of a spear.
Bathala could drive it into
the body of an animal—wild hen,
or dog, or boar—blood beating
in a thing of living flesh.

12.

The truth is
that it was a jar, not a box.
The truth is, it was beguiling
as the woman, sloping
like a pair of hips, sapphire
and rose quartz
and jasper like so many eyes
shining out of the lid.
Gathered at the bottom
we find hope pooling
under the dark.

13.

We bury our loves dreaming
one day, a century hence,
they will return as trees.

IV

CONCERNING *OBJECT PERMANENCE* AS A POETRY OF INVESTIGATION: MARGINALIA

the scientific method:
- acquire new knowledge
- correct/add to existing
  bodies of knowledge

observation
↓
problem/question
↓
hypothesis
↓
experimentation/
gathering data
↓
modify hypothesis
↓
repeat over several trials
↓
develop general theory

an observation:
I am a descendant
of doctors
with no head
for science

what makes a poem "<u>sound right</u>"?
I like finding out how things work
"I am drawn to the act of breaking things down."

Human beings
are naturally
inquisitive.

finding patterns,
establishing rhythms
making sense of things
↓
the music of the line

Mary Oliver: we "see" . . .
something about the unknown
in light of the known

                        what makes a poem
                        human? what makes
                        it intimate?

                        image → red
                        wheelbarrow
                        frog in pool, seashells
                        God's teeth
                        the gesture toward
                        the abstract
                        i.e., the unseen

the lyric poem
as "dramatic
moment"

the response
of the "I"
(no matter
how abstract)
to a situation
that compels
its speech
(no matter how
universalized)

                                        emotive/
                                        expressive
                                        function
                                        of language

emphasize: "this all makes sense in theory"

"The attempt to rationalize the world founders in the face of
   such realities as illness, death,
and suffering, whether this process of rationalization
   takes place
via scientific
inquiry or poetic
creation."

                                          the "safe" questions
                                          of what, when, where
                                          who, and how (to a
                                          limited extent)

                                          but not why

people by nature want to make sense of what happens to them—want their experiences to <u>mean something</u>, instead of simply being incidental—

how does one
proceed with poetry when
words →
diminishment (and/or
deception

depending I guess
on how charitable
you feel like being)

"poeticize" ≠ "to
make poetic" →
an implied act
of masking
↓
the glittering veil

cf. "Sonnet 74",
"Annabel Lee";
find other dead
white men who
lied to you in
grade school

"Words themselves are only human constructions."

no logic to the world
in which we live,
no harmony →
language, the means
by which that world
is ordered, founders

hypothesis:
test it
test it again
test it again
until something
gives

                                          anecdote
                                          from poetry
                                          classroom:
                                          "your speaker
                                          knows too much";

                                          "your speaker
                                          needs to be
                                          taught a lesson"

this "I" cannot abide messiness, knows nothing about
how to be messy

what do you
want to write /
about what /
in what forms

                                        what is the motivation
                                        of "knowing"
                                        in the sciences?

                                        existential anxiety
                                        cf. Lucretius

                                        Bathala → science,
                                        where "knowing" =
                                        key to agency

Can you say in your paper that what you want is to feel safe?

object permanence:
the awareness
that something
exists even if
it cannot be
perceived

why children
like peek-a-boo:
the face blinks
in and out of
existence

                                        "object permanence
is the beginning
of faith"?

                                        three acts: the book
breaks down, and is
rebuilt (sort of)

scope: natural science concepts on a basic level (grade school bio/chem/psych stuff) → medicine → grief/hope (miracles? → Jesus???)

they want you to talk about your life (?????) more (ugh)

                                                   control
                                                    ↓

                                               relinquishment?
                                               or realizing you
                                               never had it
                                               in the first place

                                             so then in what does
                                             it make sense to
                                             place our faith?

draw links:
sense of wonder /
negative capability /
the joy and also   talk about
the moral duty   loneliness
of discovery?
limits?

discuss how
science and poetry   "the collapse
traffic in metaphor   of what
                                             separates us"

last-ish part:
close-read
your own work;
"active listening"
"*in statu viatoris*"
the "laws"

why 3 and not
4, 5, 7? what
do the numbers
mean, if they
mean anything

ask →
for help
decoding
later

                                              for what and/or
                                              for whom
                                              does your "I" decide
                                              to live

"poetry is acquiescence to mystery" → you <u>must</u> submit?

ACKNOWLEDGMENTS

This manuscript was first written as a thesis project under the MA Creative Writing program at the University of the Philippines Diliman. "Considering *Object Permanence* as a Poetry of Investigation: Marginalia" derives from the exegetic essay written as part of the same project.

The poems "Scattering" and "Origin Stories" have previously been published in *Rambutan Literary* and subsequently in the journal's anthology, *Shared Horizons*. "The Heart of the Blue Whale" has previously been published in *Memoir Mixtapes*. Grateful acknowledgment is made to the editors of the aforementioned publications for giving these poems, sometimes in slightly different versions, a home in their pages.

ABOUT THE AUTHOR

Nica Bengzon is a Filipino writer with an MA in Creative Writing from the University of the Philippines, and a teacher of creative writing at the Ateneo de Manila University. Her work has been published in *Rambutan Literary* and *Memoir Mixtapes*, among others. She lives with her family in Quezon City, Metro Manila, Philippines.

ABOUT GAUDY BOY

From the Latin *gaudium*, meaning "joy," Gaudy Boy publishes books that delight readers with the various powers of art. The name is taken from the poem "Gaudy Turnout," by Singaporean poet Arthur Yap, about his time abroad in Leeds, the United Kingdom. Similarly inspired by such diasporic wanderings and migrations, Gaudy Boy brings literary works by authors of Asian heritage to the attention of an American audience and beyond. Established in 2018 as the imprint of the New York City based-literary nonprofit Singapore Unbound, we publish poetry, fiction, and literary nonfiction. Visit our website at www.singaporeunbound.org/gaudy-boy.

Winners of the Gaudy Boy Poetry Book Prize
Play for Time, by Paula Mendoza
Autobiography of Horse, by Jenifer Sang Eun Park
The Experiment of the Tropics, by Lawrence Lacambra Ypil

Fiction and Nonfiction
And the Walls Come Crumbling Down, by Tania De Rozario
The Foley Artist, by Ricco Villanueva Siasoco
Malay Sketches, by Alfian Sa'at

From Gaudy Boy Translates
Ulirát, edited by Tilde Acuña, John Bengan, Daryll Delgado, Amado Anthony G. Mendoza III, and Kristine Ong Muslim

www.ingramcontent.com/pod-product-compliance
Lightning Source LLC
Chambersburg PA
CBHW030443010526
44118CB00011B/769